This Book
Belongs To

_____

_____

_____

_____

THE CONTENTS

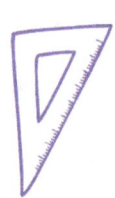      

STRATEGY FOR BACK TO SCHOOL PREPARATION

It's time to go back to school

This is a big change for you and your child,
and you may feel a lot of different things. We're here to help,
whether it's your child's first day of school or start of a new year.

There are two sections to your school toolkit:

Game Plan Part 1: 5-Step Strategy

Five easy ways to get your kid ready for the new school year are outlined here.
Both a "parent's guide" and a "kid's worksheet" are provided at each stage.

You should follow this program with your kid!
Before you begin, it's a good idea to read the entire strategy.
You'll realize how important each stage is in easing your return to school.

Game Plan Part 2: My school tools

You can use the printables, activities, and worksheets here to help your child
get ready for the problems they may experience when they start school.

There are many resources here to help your child develop important life skills,
such as the ability to solve problems independently,
speaking up when they feel wronged, learning the value of friendship,
and coping with separation anxiety.

These exercises are great for preparing your child for school
and will continue to be useful even after they've begun.
Let's start the new school year off together,
strong and prepared.

All right, here we go!

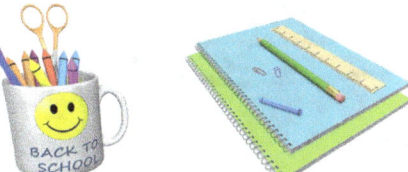   

Fill in Your Name Here!

5 STEP STRATEGY

 # Learn about your child's instructor

Your child will feel safest with their instructor when they are not with you. They will feel more comfortable and at home in the classroom if they have a good relationship with their teacher.

To children, those with whom they share a sense of "sameness" provide a sense of closeness and community. Your child will feel closer and more connected to their teacher when they can identify shared similarities with that person. Even if it's just a little thing like:

"Both your teacher and you have a brother!"

To assist you and your child's teacher get to know each other better before school starts, here are some questions to consider asking:

Are you an only child?

Are there any pets in your home?

Thirdly, which color do you like best?

Which subject do you enjoy teaching the most?

There are more ways to make your youngster feel more comfortable in class:

❖ Ask the teacher to send your child a picture of himself or herself.

❖ Tell your child about your favorite teachers when you were young.

If you can't get in touch with the teacher, that's fine! You can help your child write down their thoughts, worries, or things they are curious about. They can put these in their backpacks and bring them to the first day of school to ask the teacher. Practice answering the questions out loud to help your child feel surer of himself or herself Coming up to the teacher.

LEARN ABOUT MY INSTRUCTOR

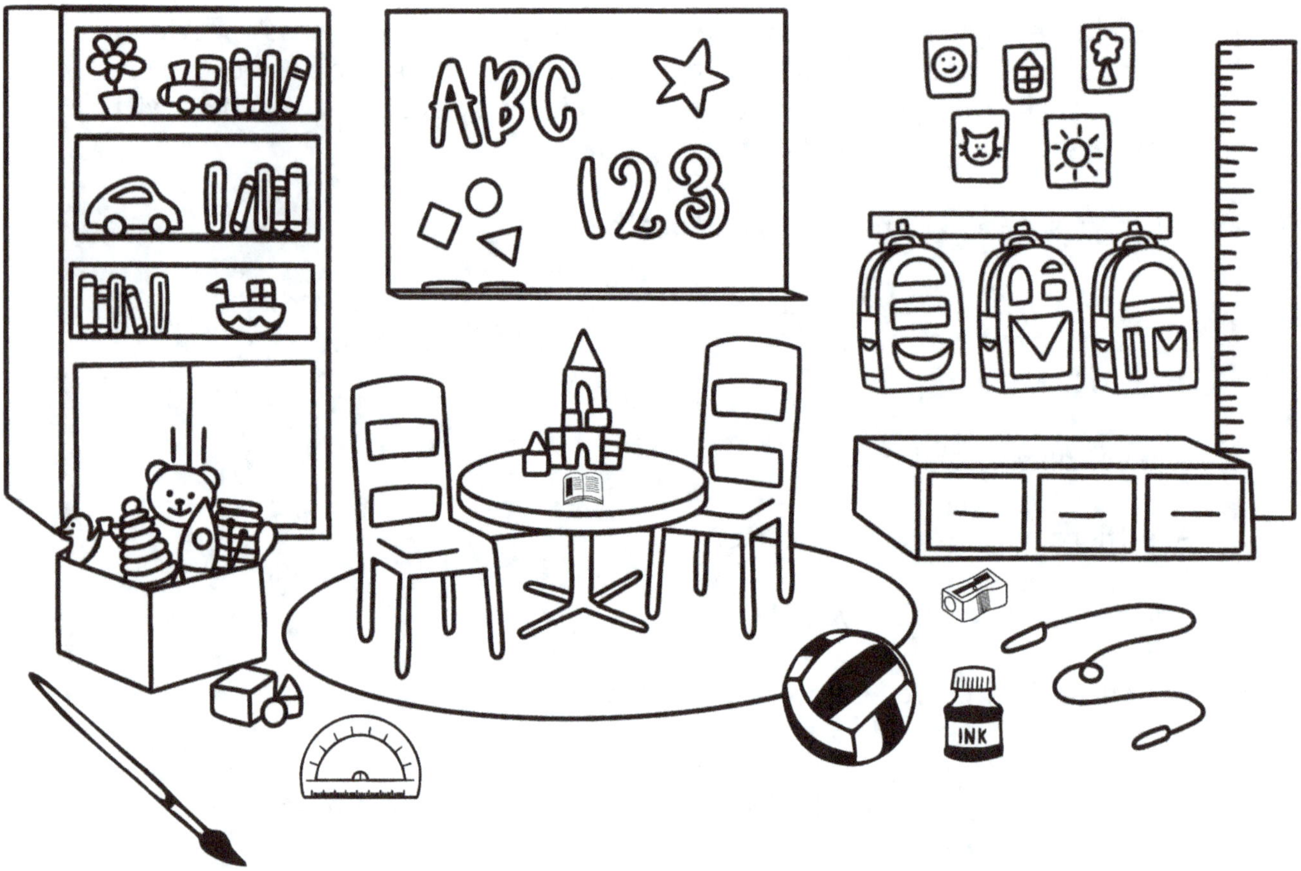

ADVICE TO CARE GIVERS

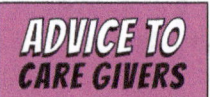

Encourage your kid to express their excitement about the first day of school by coloring in this picture and drawing themselves and their instructor in the classroom. After they are done coloring, inquire about their impressions of the artwork.

 **Learn about your school**

Starting school may be both joyful and frightening for children.

Help your child prepare for the first day of school by showing them pictures of the school, their classroom, and the entrance.

Here are some suggestions for easing your child into the new school year and boosting his or her self-assurance.

1. Take a drive by your child's school and show them the layout, where recess will be held, and the entrance they'll use on their first day.

2. You should park at the school and let your kid run about the grounds to become used to the environment.

3. Third, talk to your kid's teacher about getting images of the classroom. Describe the various work spaces, including desks and cubbies.

4. Use the "Get to Know My School!" document to have your kid design a picture of their future classroom.

 It's fine if you don't have access to your kid's school to take pictures. Take your kid online and have a look at some photographs of classrooms.

DISCOVER MY SCHOOL

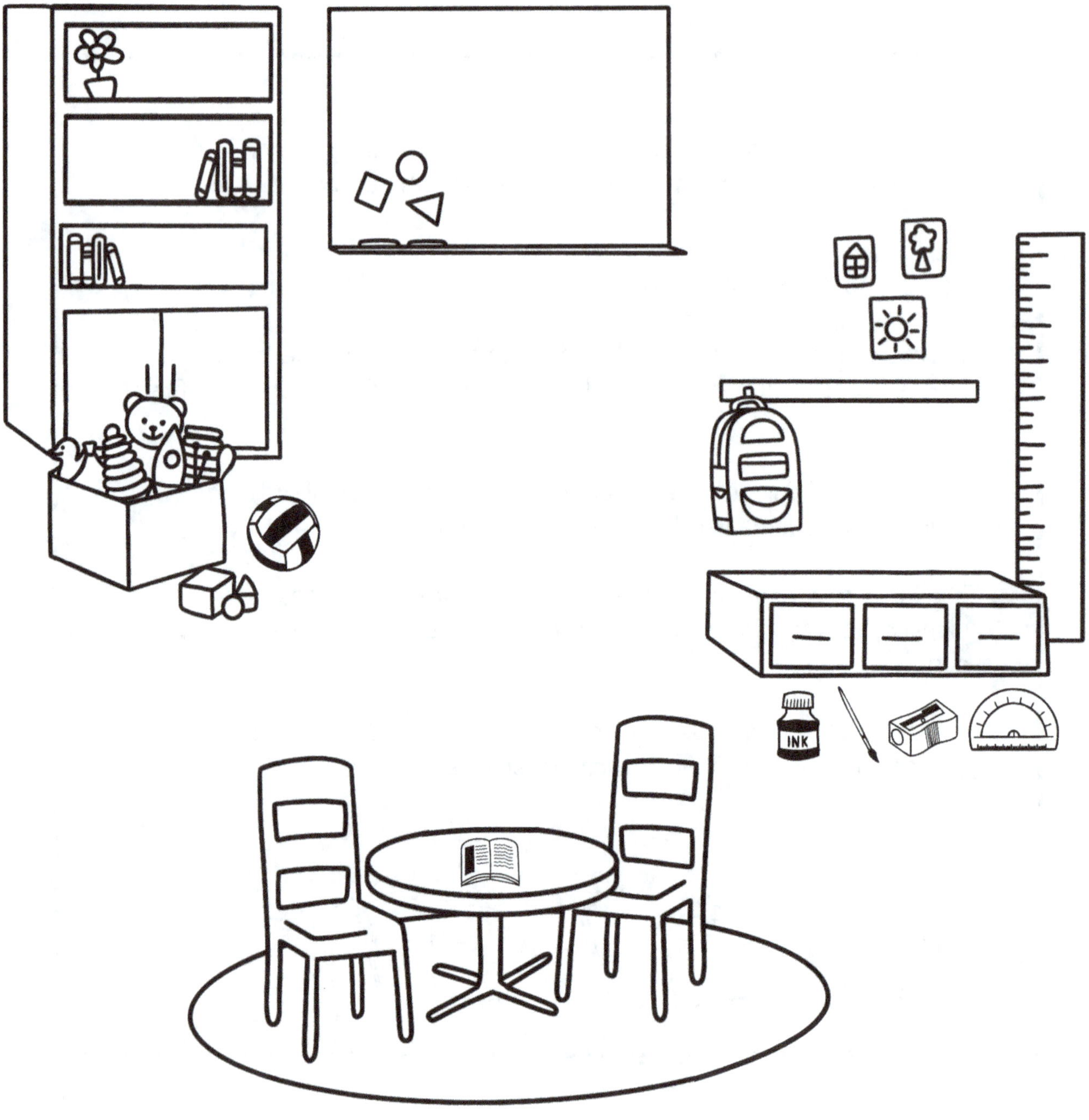

ADVICE TO CARE GIVERS

To help your kid visualize their future classroom, we've provided a handy worksheet.

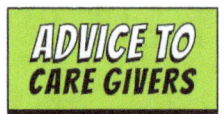

 **Recognize your routine**

With all the new experiences and challenges that come with starting school, it is beneficial for children to have a routine they can rely on to help them feel secure and confident as they navigate their day.

1

Make sure your kid is prepared for the day by establishing a set of morning rituals.

A few examples:

a. Pack a lunch;
b. Select an outfit;
c. Consume breakfast;
d. Don hiking gear.

2

Help your youngster adjust to new settings by establishing a routine for after school.

For instance:

a. Putting away lunch,
b. Eating a snack,
c. Having some quiet time,
d. Reading,
e. Playing outside

3

Develop a relaxing bedtime ritual to help your kid unwind at the end of the day.

For example:

a. Rough and tumble play
b. Bath or shower
c. Brush teeth
d. Put on pajamas
e. Read books

 **ADVICE TO CARE GIVERS** Start going over the new routines with your child at least a week before school starts to help them get used to the change. It can be helpful to talk about the changes and act out your new habits.

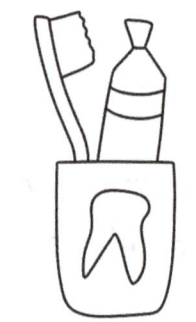

Have I brushed my teeth?

Have I have breakfast?

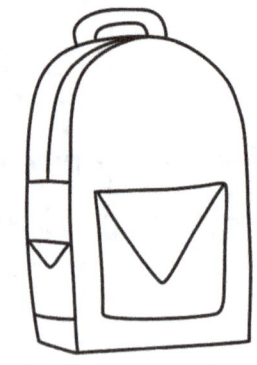

Is my backpack packed?

MY CHECKLIST FOR THE MORNING!

Is a coat required?

Is my lunch ready?

Did I bid farewell to my family?

Is my attire appropriate?

3   Learn the route to school

Here are some tips to help you be ready for your child's commute to school, whether they take the bus, walk, or you drive them.

Traveling by Bus:

Together, practice strolling to the bus stop.
Discuss bus safety. Here are some things you should teach your child:

- ❖ Please wait for the bus to come to a complete stop before approaching it.
- ❖ You must remain seated throughout the entire ride.
- ❖ Please don't sit on the aisles.
- ❖ Don't lean out the bus window; stay inside the vehicle at all times.
- ❖ When riding the bus, your bus driver is the responsible adult in charge.
- ❖ If you're worried about your safety on the bus, you can tell them.

Assist your child in learning some useful skills for the bus.
For instance:

- ❖ Speak with friends
- ❖ Read a book
- ❖ Play with a soothing object (stuffed animal, fidget toy, etc.).

*Find out if your school has practice riding the bus!

Via Foot to School:

Try walking together to school! Tell them where you'll leave them.

Talk about the rules for road safety. Some of the things you'll need to teach your child:

- ❖ Listen to what the crossing guard says.
- ❖ Before crossing, look both ways.

Tell your child who they might see on their way to school and who they might walk with.

- ❖ Do what the crossing guard tells you. Before crossing, look in both directions.
- ❖ For example, crossing guards will help you cross the street. They will be holding a stop sign and have a bright vest on.

Going to School by Car:

Drive to school with them and show them where you'll drop them off.

If your school has a carpool lane, describe how it will work for them.

Discuss the after-school pickup plan and ask if they have any questions.

Set up chairs in your house to look like a bus! Have your child act out going to the bus stop. Then, help your child think of some things to say to start a conversation on the bus.

THE ROUTE I TAKE TO GET TO SCHOOL!

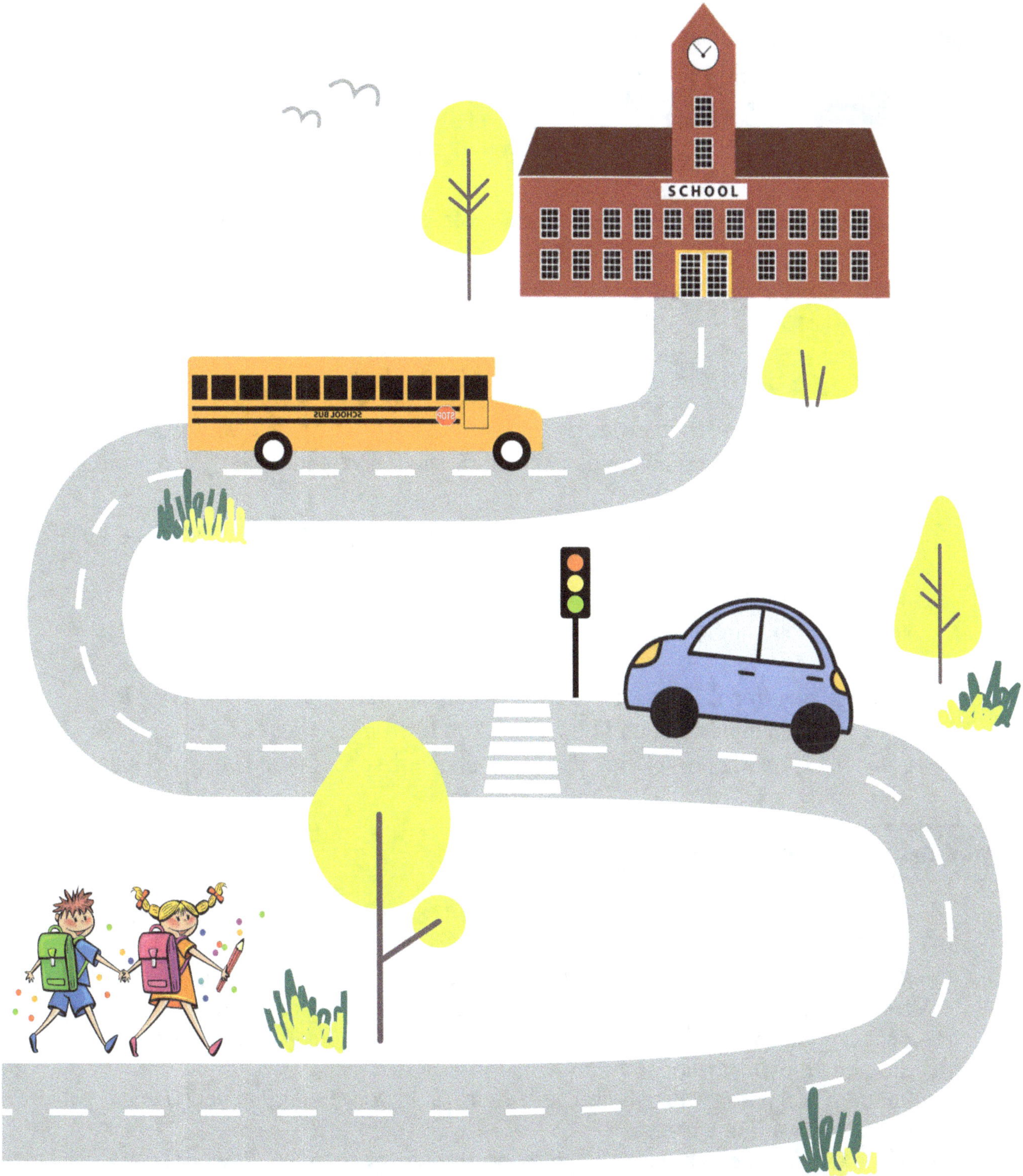

ADVICE TO CARE GIVERS

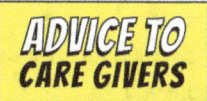

You can get to school in a variety of ways! Have your child draw a map to school, marking the routes they plan to take. Use this as a springboard to discuss the questions and topics introduced on the previous page.

5 Find out how we are linked even when we are apart

Here are some things you can do to help with the school separation:

1. Tell them what is going to happen:

❖ "When we walk to school, I'll drop you off at the front door, give you two bear hugs, and then leave."

❖ "I'll walk you to the bus stop and wait for you there until the bus arrives." You'll take the bus to school, while I'll go to work."

❖ "After school, I'll be waiting for you at the bus stop to greet you with a big bear hug!"

2. Build bridges between yourself and your child:

❖ Assist them in locating objects of comfort to grasp or grip when they are missing you. This can be a plush animal in their backpack or a tiny pebble in their pocket.

❖ Make matching bracelets and let them know they can pull on them to let you know they're missing them shall convey to you their want of you.

❖ Tell them you two are connected by an invisible thread. Tell them to visualize you pulling the thread back and to tug on it whenever they miss you.

❖ Trace a tiny heart into both of your hands so that when they look at it, they will remember you and how much you both miss them.

❖ Look for a family photo that they may show at school and give you a kiss on when they need to.

Make it a memorable reunion by:

❖ Share your joy by saying something like, "I'm very glad to see you! Have a wonderful evening!

❖ Remind them how much you've missed spending time with them: "I've been thinking about you all day!" Oh, I'm so happy that you're back!

❖ Encourage conversation by saying, "I missed you today!" When asked, "What did you enjoy most about today?"

❖ Recount a time of triumph and tell them, "I'm very proud of you! Today, you rode the bus like a pro!

❖ Act excited: "You're home!" I'm dying to hear about your day because I've missed you so much.

ADVICE TO CARE GIVERS Before your child goes to school all day, try small separations with them. Practice using some of your bridges when there isn't much time between them, like when you're at Grandma's house for a few hours. This helps your child get used to the idea of being apart from you.

NO MATTER HOW FAR APART MY PARENT AND I ARE, WE ARE ALWAYS IN TOUCH

ADVICE TO CARE GIVERS Reassure your child that your heart remains attached to them even while you are apart. Have your kid follow the path of the unseen thread that links you two. Have them pull this rope and see you pulling back if they need a reminder of you.

IS IT TIME FOR SCHOOL?

ADVICE TO CARE GIVERS Ask your child if they have any more topics they would like to discuss before school starts, after they have completed the 5 Step Plan. Before they leave for school, ask them to illustrate some of the things they are looking forward to using this worksheet!

(14)

MY SCHOOL TOOLS

AMAZING ME

Hello, my name is:

This is a photo of me:

My age is: _____

I was born on:

_____

The one thing about me I adore

One way I'm nice is:

_____

_____

_____

I feel loved when:

My favorite activity is:

Influential Individuals to me:

What I Did Today:
Nurture Jar Questions

Put these questions in a jar or bowl after you've cut them out. Go around the table at dinner and ask each person to answer a question. This is a fun way to find out about your child's day and show that you care about how they are doing.

Friend Inquiries

Which of your pals attended class today?

Friend Inquiries

What did you do in school?

Friend Inquiries

Did any of your buddies say or do anything amusing today?

Friend Inquiries

Is anyone you know feeling down?

Culinary Questions

What did you eat today
for a snack?

Culinary Questions

What kind of food did the kids
have today?

Culinary Questions

What did you eat for
lunch today?

Culinary Questions

Which of today's meals did
you enjoy the most?

Question Game

What kind of games did
you play today?

Question Game

What was the most enjoyable
thing you did today?

Question Game

With which toys
did you play?

Question Game

Have you encountered any
unappealing games today?

Feeling Questions

Is there anything that made
you joyful today?

Feeling Questions

Was there anything that
confused you?

Feeling Questions

How did (caregiver's name)
feel today?

Feeling Questions

Today, did anything
tricky happen?

Questions about Learning

Did you discover anything
new today?

Questions about Learning

Did you do anything
wrong today?

Questions about Learning

What's something new
you tried today?

Questions about Learning

Is there anything specific about
which you're curious?

Your Own Concern

Your Own Concern

Write a letter to your kid

Writing your child a love letter is a wonderful method to show your affection when you are apart. Help your youngster express themselves artistically while you talk about your shared humanity. Then, you can spring a surprise on your kid by placing a letter in their lunch box. When they go home, you can question them about it.

At this very moment, you are in my thoughts. When you arrive home, please know how much I anticipate seeing you.

I hope your lunch goes well today. You are the best!

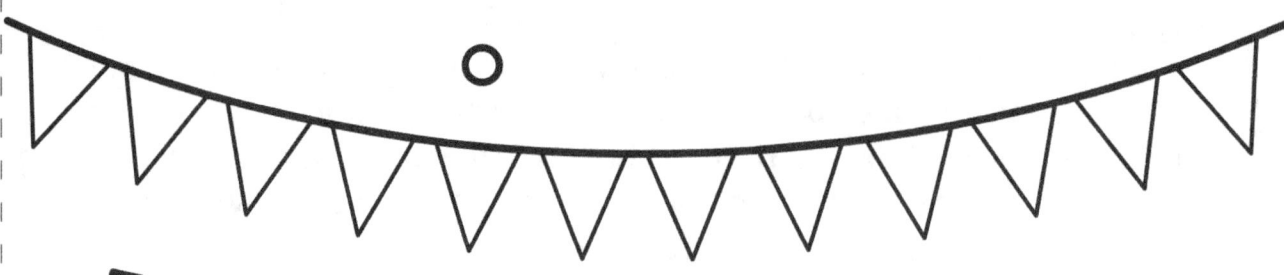

I can't wait to hear about everything you did today.
If things get hard, know that when you get home
I will give you a big bear hug.

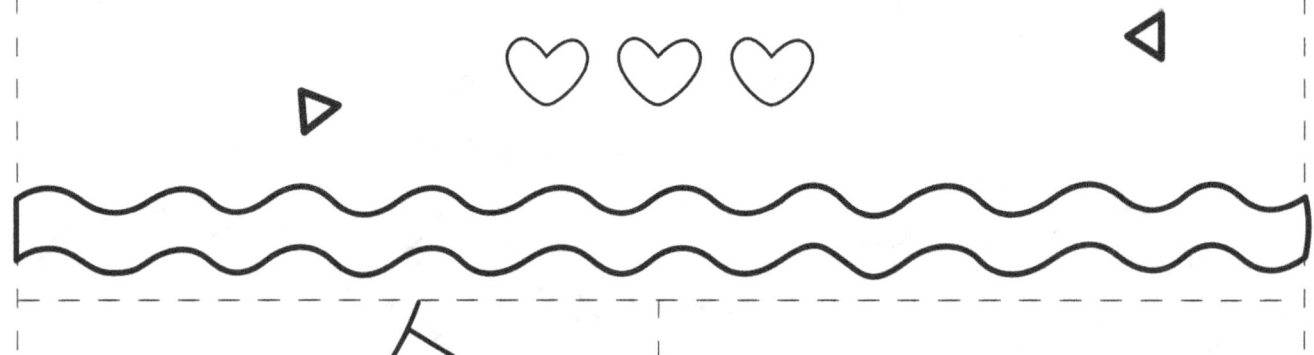

You are STRONG.
You're NICE.
You KNOW A LOT.
You are UNIQUE!

The gold pot at the end
of my rainbow is you!

Your smile is the most beautiful thing you have on.

Incredibly **happy** for you

You are the most important thing in my life ♥

Nothing you could ever do could ever change my love for you.

You shine more brightly than any star in the sky.

Star of the show,

no matter where you go,

you will always be loved and admired.

I hope to see you at home later.

We're going to settle in

and take a deep breath. Believe in yourself;

you have the strength and bravery

to see this through.

What am I able to manage at school?

Acting kindly

What I think
and how I feel

What I will do
in the future

Assisting others

Doing my best.

I'm keeping my
hands to myself.

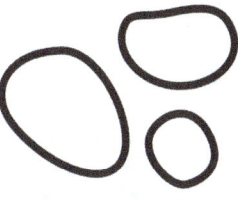

Using my tools
to calm down

THE THINGS I CAN'T MANAGE:

Condition
of the
atmosphere

The actions
and words
of others

Things that
have previously
occurred

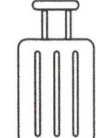

One of my
closest friends
recently
relocated

After
tripping
over my
shoelace

Stats:
age, height,
and hair
shade

Things will happen at school that your kid can't prevent. This could be a challenge for them!
You can use this worksheet to talk to your kid about what they have control over
and what they don't.

(25)

What should I do? Wheel for solving problems

Is there a minor issue you think I might be able to help with?
Several answers are provided below.

Get them to stop

STOP

Get over it

Change your plans.

Inhale deeply.

Talk to a responsible adult about serious issues.

"I Feel..."

Put in a "I" message

Get some rest.

Discuss and swap roles

Exchange views

 **ADVICE TO CARE GIVERS** If your kid is having issues at school (or at home), you can help them out by talking through the options on this wheel. Talk to your kid about what kinds of examples could work best for them.

What should I do? Wheel for solving problems

Is there a minor issue you think I might be able to help with?
How would YOU solve the problem?

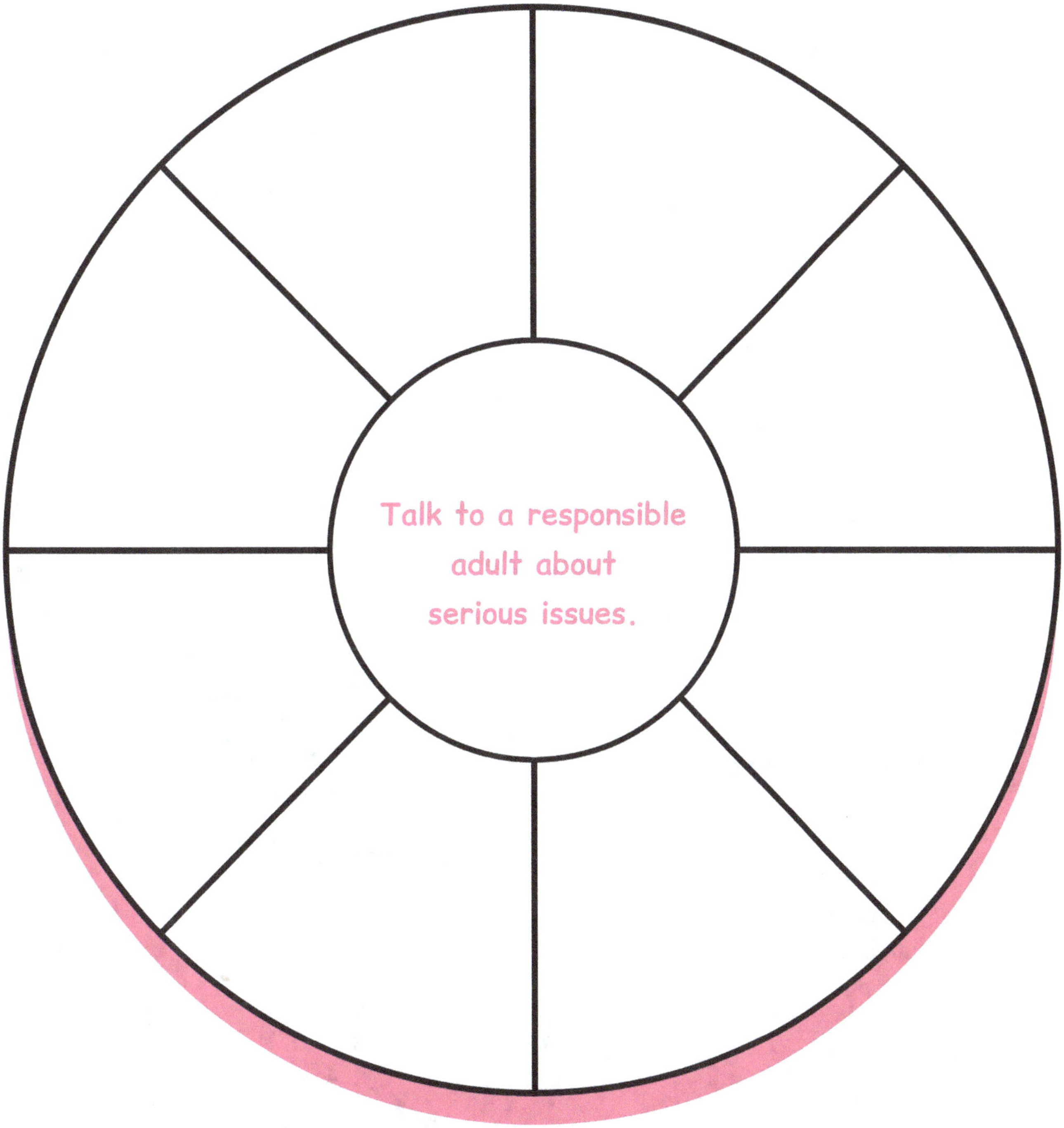

Talk to a responsible adult about serious issues.

 **ADVICE TO CARE GIVERS** Use this worksheet to assist your child come up with potential solutions to problems they may encounter at school (or at home).

What saying farewell is difficult,
I can recall the following:

"My mom or dad can kiss my hand and save it for later."

"The love my parents have for me is indescribable. What they come up with me all along that day!"

"There's a magical thread that binds me to my mom and dad! If I end up missing them, all I have to do is pull on it."

"Adults never forget the children they raised. They keep coming back!"

ADVICE TO CARE GIVERS

Color this page with your child to show them that you're always thinking about them, even when you're not with them. Your child can even take this page to school with them to remind them of you on days when they miss you.

(28)

I possess a powerful voice

Suppose My Friend...

Uses up my favorite toy.

Hits me on the schoolyard

Plans something that seems dangerous.

Meanly says something

Propose a hug

Asks to look at my private parts

I Can Tell...

Stop. My physical well-being is under my control.

I don't want a hug, thanks.

This plan doesn't make me feel safe. This is not something I will do.

I own that. Could I get it back?

No, I have control over my body.

You can be upset with me if you want to, but you can't be mean.

Your kid has incredible power in their voice. Your youngster may learn how to use their powerful voice in each situation by tracing the lines. You can also play a role in the scenarios with your child to help them practice speaking up.

Good Companions:

Help one another

Complement one another

Hear each other out

Have a good time

Take it in turns

Are kind to one another

ADVICE TO
CARE GIVERS

Children often struggle while attempting to forge friendships. Look at the many scenarios and talk to your kid about how they can be a better friend.

My after-school relaxation strategy

Request a hug.

Take three deep breathes.

Count to ten

Have some fun with blocks.

Make a puzzle

Have a bite to eat

Snuggle up on the sofa.

Tell someone how I'm feeling.

Squeeze my teddy bear

ADVICE TO CARE GIVERS School is a time when kids put on their best behavior and try to suppress their feelings. Many people, upon returning home, require an outlet for the pent-up emotions they've been experiencing. This poster of stress-reduction techniques might serve as a helpful reminder to your activities that allow them to release pent-up emotions and relax after a long day at school.